D0563812

Other books in this series:
A Feast of After Dinner Jokes   A Portfolio of Business Jokes
A Round of Golf Jokes   A Romp of Naughty Jokes
A Spread of Over 40's Jokes   A Binge of Diet Jokes
A Tankful of Motoring Jokes   A Knockout of Sports Jokes
A Triumph of Over 50s Jokes

Published in the USA in 1992 by Exley Giftbooks
Published in Great Britain in 1992 by Exley Publications Ltd

12 11 10 9 8 7 6 5 4

Cartoons © Bill Stott 1992. Copyright © Helen Exley 1992.
ISBN 1-85015-320-5

A copy of the CIP data is available from the British Library on request.
All rights reserved. No part of this publication may be reproduced or
transmitted in any form or by any means, electronic or mechanical,
including photocopy, recording or any information storage and retrieval
system without permission in writing from the Publisher.

Series editor: Helen Exley.
Editor: Elizabeth Cotton.

We dedicate this to Sara and Jeff: Be Happy!

Jokes by Walter Kanitz reproduced by permission of the Canadian Publishers, McClelland & Stewart.
Jokes by Peter Eldin reproduced by permission of Cassell Plc. Material from ". . . And Finally" by Martin
Lewis reproduced by permission of Hutchinson. Jokes by Kevin Goldstein-Jackson reproduced by
permission of Elliot Right Way Books. Jokes by Herbert V. Prochnow and Herbert V. Prochnow Jr and
Stuart Turner reproduced by permission of Harper Collins. Jokes by Barry Wogan and Barbara Jeffrey
reproduced by permission of Foulsham. Extracts from The Return of Heroic Failures by Stephen Pile
reproduced by permission of Rogers, Coleridge & White Ltd. Material from The Guinness Book of
Marriage © Valerie Porter 1991 Published by Guinness Publishing Ltd, Enfield.

Cover designed by The Pinpoint Design Company.
Printed by Kossuth Printing House Co. in Hungary.

Exley Publications Ltd, 16 Chalk Hill, Watford, Herts WD1 4BN, United Kingdom.
Exley Giftbooks, 232 Madison Avenue, Suite 1206, NY10016, USA.

—A BOUQUET OF—
WEDDING
·JOKES·

Cartoons by Bill Stott

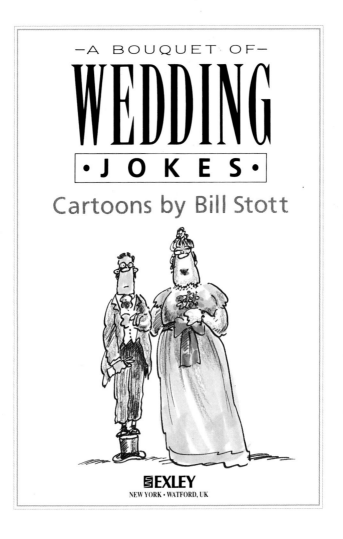

EXLEY
NEW YORK · WATFORD, UK

My bridegroom's first words to me at the altar
when I joined him were: "Who are you?" It made me
think that the hours I spent on myself before going to
church were all worth while.

from a letter in the *Daily Mail*

*

"In Sheffield, England, the groom tripped over
the bride's extra-long train and sprained his ankle. The
officiating clergyman got tangled up in it and fell,
suffering a painful back injury. But when the best man
tripped over the train and banged his head hard against
the altar, the enraged father of the bride produced a
pocket knife and sliced the offending train off."

WALTER KANITZ, from *The Speaker's Book*

*

Newspaper Misprint "...the bride wore a Spanish
influenced dress with high neck, and frills on the
sleeves...The dress which was gathered at the back
gently fell to the floor."

Quoted in the *Middlesex Advertiser and Gazette*

THE BRIDE OVERSLEPT...

THE BRIDE'S MOTHER'S NOT HAVING THE BEST

OF DAYS SO FAR...

The Family Come Too

In villages in Pakistan, a prospective bridegroom is brought before relatives of the bride, who insult him with every known invective. The theory is that, if he can take that, he has nothing to fear from what the bride will say later.

*

The young bride was extremely nervous before her wedding. Convinced that she would make some terrible mistake during the ceremony, she asked her mother for advice. "It's quite simple," she told her. "Just remember that you walk down the AISLE, stand at the ALTAR and then we sing a HYMN."

Reassured by this, the bride arrived at the church on the morning of her wedding - repeating her mother's words over and over to herself. As she made her way down the aisle the guests could hear her saying to herself what sounded suspiciously like "I'll alter him."!

*

AW, COME ON GERRY - I'M YOUR BEST MAN - WOULD I LEAVE

YOU THERE ALL NIGHT?

THE WORST BEST MAN

Choosing the right sort of best man is the key to the smooth running of a wedding ceremony. In 1920 Albert Muldoon agreed to be the best man for his good friend Christopher and what a wise choice he proved to be.

At the service in Kileter parish church Mr. Muldoon wasted no time in standing on the wrong side of the groom. So, when the priest began the service he naturally addressed his questions to Albert, having never seen the happy couple before.

As Christopher was understandably nervous and tongue-tied on this great occasion, Albert answered for him. Only at the signing of the register, when the best man was putting his name under the space marked "groom" at the priest's direction, did the bride object.

Thanks to the best man the ceremony was doubly memorable for the couple because they had to do the whole thing again.

STEPHEN PILE, from *The Return of Heroic Failures*

*

GOODBYE FREEDOM

"Marriage is a great institution, but I'm not ready for an institution yet."

MAE WEST

*

"I had no need to marry. I had three pets at home which answered the same purpose as a husband. I have a dog which growls every morning, a parrot which swears all the afternoon, and a cat which comes home late at night."

MARIE CORRELLI

*

"Marriage: the state or condition of a community consisting of a master, a mistress, and two slaves, making, in all, two."

AMBROSE BIERCE

*

"Marriage has many pains but celibacy has no pleasures."

SAMUEL JOHNSON

*

AND YOU'RE BOTH ABSOLUTELY SURE ABOUT THIS?

THE BRIDE THAT GOT AWAY

A very pretty young woman had a persistent but unwanted suitor in a nearby town. When she broke off their relationship he wouldn't take no for an answer and bombarded her with love letters and deliveries of flowers and presents. This postal assault continued for three months until it finally produced results. The young woman eloped with the mail man!

*

"A Yugoslavian man arranged to elope with his young girlfriend and, as they'd planned, spirited her away from her home, wrapped in a blanket. He put her in his car and drove speedily away. Only after he was some miles away did he stop to greet his beloved - but when he pulled the blanket back he discovered that he'd abducted her seventy-three-year-old grandmother. What's more the old lady took advantage of his state of shock to beat him up!"

from *Comic Speeches for Social Occasions*

*

MESSAGE FROM THE BRIDE - SHE DEVELOPED A HUGE ZIT ON THE END OF HER NOSE OVERNIGHT AND WOULD YOU MIND TRYING AGAIN NEXT SATURDAY?

SORRY ABOUT THIS - I'VE NEVER DONE A CIRCUS

WEDDING BEFORE...

The elderly minister became confused at the wedding service because of the groom's long hair. Then he smiled and said: "Ah, will one of you please kiss the bride."

ROY BOLITHO

*

The Hollywood film actress was getting married for the seventh time when the clergyman stumbled over the words of the ceremony.

"It's all right," hissed the actress. "Take it again from the top of page five."

KEVIN GOLDSTEIN-JACKSON, from *Jokes for Telling*

*

When planning their wedding the young couple asked their vicar if he approved of sex before marriage.

"Certainly not!," came the reply, "it would delay the service."

PATRICIA MACDONALD

*

At a village wedding the vicar gave out the final hymn:

"Hymn number 540." There was no response from the organist who had turned round towards the vicar and shook his head at him.

The vicar, knowing something was amiss, looked at his sheet.

"Sorry," he said, "hymn number 520. 'Love divine, all love excelling'." Hymn number 540 was 'Fight the good fight with all thy might'.

MAJOR-GENERAL JOHN GALBRAITH GILL, CBE, DSO, MC
from *Pass the Port Again*

*

"Which reminds me of the story of a best man who was asked to read from the Bible as part of his speech 1 John 4:18 'There is no fear in love, but perfect love casts out fear.'

Unfortunately, he read from the Gospel of John 4:18, where it says 'You have had five husbands, and he whom you now have is not your husband!'"

BARBARA JEFFERY, from *Wedding Speeches and Toasts*

WHEN YOUR GRANDMOTHER VOLUNTEERED TO DO THE MUSIC -
I THOUGHT SHE PLAYED THE ORGAN!

AND CAN WE BOOK THE CHRISTENING NOW, PLEASE?

"Vows are exchanged at every wedding. Although the words have been uttered millions of times, no one ever gets them right:

You say 'I do' when it's not your turn.

You mispronounce your name.

You mispronounce your spouse's name.

You don't mispronounce anyone's name, because you're too terrified to pronounce anything.

There are two defences against the embarrassment of fumbled vows. One is an extremely loud organist. The other is elopement."

from *The Unofficial Newly Weds' Handbook*

*

Small girl: "Daddy why do people have sixteen marriage partners?"

Father: "Whatever gave you that idea?"

Small girl: "At cousin Sarah's wedding the vicar said they could have sixteen partners - four better, four worse, four richer and four poorer."

Mr. and Mrs. Simon Peters
request the honour
of your presents
at the marriage of their daughter Eve
to Mr. James Johnson.

Wedding invitation, quoted in *The Best of Shrdlu*

*

"Young farmer with one hundred acres would
be pleased to hear from young lady with tractor.
Please send photograph of tractor."

Advertisement in *Eversham Admag*, 1977

*

"Due to a misunderstanding over the
telephone we stated that the couple would live at the
home of the bridegroom's father. We have been
asked to point out that they will in fact live
at the Old Manse."

Quoted in *The Black and White Misprint Show* by Fritz Spiegl

HAPPY, DARLING?

*

"Immediately after the ceremony the bride and
bridegroom go into the vestry and sigh."

Women's Magazine, quoted in *The Best of Shrdlu*

SORRY I'M LATE - I DASHED HOME AND GOT CHANGED - THE
FROCK JUST DIDN'T FEEL RIGHT.

And Then There's The Groom . . .

Happy groom: "Oh my little snuggle bunny I'm so proud that you've agreed to be my wife! Just think you'll be putting up with my ugly old mug for the rest my life."

His new bride: "Don't worry, honey - most days you'll be out at work until it gets dark!"

M.C.G.

*

She was sixteen, he was seventeen, and the parents were opposed to their wedding. But they couldn't prevent it without making a scene, so they agreed to it. When the officiating clergyman asked the bridegroom to repeat after him "With all my worldly goods I thee endow," his father nudged his wife and whispered, "There goes his motor scooter."

HERBERT V. PROCHNOW AND HERBERT V. PROCHNOW JR.
from *Jokes, Quotes and One-liners*

*

Smile Please!

"The riot squad was called out when a pitched battle developed during a wedding in Naples. The bride fainted and eleven guests had to be taken to hospital by ambulances. The trouble started when the two sets of in-laws could not agree who should be photographed first together with the newly-weds."

WALTER KANITZ, from *The Speaker's Book*

*

"Look pleasant please!" requested the photographer as he tried to organize the relatives of the happy couple for the group photograph. "As soon as I've taken the picture you can resume your natural expressions!"

YOU RUN AND GET IT WHILE I CHANGE THE FILM...

THE BATTERED BRIDEGROOM

"Everything is so hectic," sighed the young bride who was to be married at the end of the week. "What with organizing the flowers, choosing the organ music, setting out the seating plan - I'm just frightened that we'll overlook some insignificant little detail." "Don't worry dear," replied her mother, "I'll see that he gets there."

*

As a "new man" I'm sure the groom will be doing his share of the cooking. Last time I had dinner with him I was so impressed that I've bought him a carving set as a wedding present - three chisels and a mallet!

*

I asked her father if I could marry her and he said, "Just leave your name and address and we'll notify you if nothing better comes up."

PETER ELDIN, from *Jokes and Quotes for Speeches*

*THE VICAR SAYS CONFETTI MAKES LESS OF A MESS IF YOU
LEAVE IT IN THE BOX...*

SO WHAT IS MARRIAGE?

"Marriage is the alliance of two people, one of whom never remembers birthdays and the other never forgets them."

OGDEN NASH

*

"Marriage is a sort of friendship recognised by the police."

ROBERT LOUIS STEVENSON

*

"Marriage is popular because it combines the maximum of temptation with the maximum of opportunity."

GEORGE BERNARD SHAW

"Marriage may often be a stormy lake, but celibacy is almost always a muddy horse-pond."

THOMAS LOVE PEACOCK

*

"Marriage is the deep, deep peace of the double-bed after the hurly burly of the chaise longue."

MRS. PATRICK CAMPBELL

YOU'D BETTER STOP... THE BRIDE'S MOTHER HAS JUST THROWN

UP IN THE CHIEF USHER'S TOP HAT...

"My mother always finds fault with the girls I bring home," confided Brian to his old schoolfriend. "She says that they're either too clever or too silly, too pretty or too plain, too chatty or too shy, too fat or too thin. I can never please her!"

"The only solution," advised his friend, "is to search until you find a girl exactly like your mother - then she won't be able to pick fault with her!"

Six months later Brian bumped into the same old friend who asked him how his love life was going.

"I followed your advice," said Brian sadly. "I searched and searched and eventually I found a girl just like my mother - same personality, same height, same weight - same everything!"

"What went wrong?"

"My father hated her."

E. H. COTTON

*

You're not losing a daughter, you're gaining a son. In my case I'm also gaining a bathroom.

*

<u>POOR OLD DAD</u>

The father watching his daughter select a very expensive wedding gown: "I don't mind giving you away, but must I gift wrap you, too?"

HERBERT V. PROCHNOW AND HERBERT V. PROCHNOW JR.

TERRY? I THINK YOU MAY HAVE YOUR DAD'S SUIT...

*YES, I'M BLOTTO... MY FEET HURT, MY SON-IN-LAW'S
A TWERP AND THIS DO'S COST ME TEN GRAND - I'M ENTITLED
TO GET BLOTTO.*

*

"At a wedding I went to recently a collection plate
was passed around the church during the service -
very unusual I know, but apparently the bride's
father requested it!"

M.C.G.

*

OOH LOOK - THEIR FIRST TIFF...

WAR IS DECLARED

There are only two times in a man's life when he can't understand a woman - before marriage and after marriage!

ANONYMOUS

*

"If you think women are the weaker sex...try pulling the sheets back to your side."

STUART TURNER, from *The Public Speaker's Bible*

*

A husband is a man who'll stick by you in all the troubles you wouldn't have had if you hadn't married him.

*

"All marriages are happy. It's the living together afterward that causes all the trouble."

RAYMOND HULL

*

DID YOU WIN THE BET?

MOTHER'S BIG DAY . . .

The woman wearing an enormous flowery hat was stopped at the entrance to the church by one of the ushers.

"Are you a friend of the bride?" he asked.

"Of course not!" snapped the woman. "I'm the groom's mother."

KEVIN GOLDSTEIN-JACKSON, from *Joke after Joke after Joke*

"Every bride has to learn it's not her wedding but her mother's."

LUCI JOHNSON NUGENT

I KNOW IT'S AN OLD JOKE, BUT IT SEEMS TO HAVE HAPPENED TO OUR MOTHERS.

SHSHH! YOUR FATHER'S NEARLY FINISHED

TOMORROW'S SPEECH...

"It usually takes me more than three weeks to prepare a good impromptu speech."

MARK TWAIN

*

The bride's father was nervous at the prospect of proposing the first toast at his daughter's wedding. As the guests began to finish their meal, he started to shuffle together the pages of his carefully-prepared speech and get himself ready for the dreaded ordeal. The master of ceremonies came up beside him and whispered in his ear, "Would you like to start your speech now, sir, or shall we allow the guests to continue enjoying themselves for a while longer?"

*

After his rather lengthy speech the bride's father was talking to one of his guests.

"How did you find my speech?" he asked.

"Oh, very refreshing - very refreshing indeed," came the reply.

"Did you really?" he asked reassured.

"Oh yes, I felt like a new person when I woke up!"

A Good Time Was Had By All . . .

Newly-weds John and Barbara Besio claimed this record at the Blue Dolphin restaurant in Los Angeles during 1980.

The reception made a promising start when the groom's father expressed the wish to dance upon the table. So unbridled was this performance that the manager called the police. In the resulting fracas five policemen were injured and six wedding guests were arrested.

At this point the bride asked what kind of family she was marrying into, whereupon the groom departed from the usual custom, picked up the entire wedding cake and pushed it in her face. When fighting broke out between the happy couple, the police were called again and threatened to arrest them. Guests waving off the newly-weds in the going-

YOUR MOTHER'S JUST CHECKING THAT NO ONE TAKES

TWO CHICKEN LEGS...

*

away car noticed that Mrs. Besio, as we
must now call her, landed a blow which
appeared to temporarily stun her
husband, bringing peace to an otherwise
perfect occasion.

STEPHEN PILE, from *The Return of Heroic Failures*

Unaccustomed As I Am. . .

"The brain is a wonderful thing. It never stops functioning from the time you're born until the moment you stand up to make a speech."

HERBERT V. PROCHNOW AND HERBERT V. PROCHNOW JR.

*

Two of the groom's elderly aunts were delighted to attend the wedding of their much-loved nephew. After the wedding ceremony the guests assembled for the reception. The bride's father was the first to give a speech of congratulations. He was a lovely man and very fond of his daughter, but his speech went on and on and on - for what seemed like hours. The elder of the two aunts, who was a little deaf, leant over to her sister and said, "Hasn't he finished yet?" to which the other replied in a loud and clear voice, "Yes, he's finished, but he doesn't seem able to stop."

E. H. COTTON

*

AND I WELL REMEMBER - WHEN OUR LOUISE WAS THREE - OR

PERHAPS THREE AND A HALF...

THE LEAST SUCCESSFUL WEDDING CAKE

Your wedding is a day to remember and Signor Enrico Faldini of Naples is unlikely to forget his. At the reception during 1981 the wedding cake exploded when a waiter was lighting the candles with the result that two guests, two waiters and a tourist taking a photograph of Signora Faldini were treated for shock.

Credit goes to the chef who later said: "I think I must have used too much alcohol in the mix."

STEPHEN PILE, from *The Return of Heroic Failures*

APPARENTLY, THE BRIDE'S AUNT, WHO IS FILTHY RICH AND

NINETY-EIGHT YEARS OF AGE, MADE THE CAKE...

*

"The bride's mother made the cake from a
powerful recipe which has been in the family for
generations - known as 'The gateau-blaster!' "

Amazing Weddings

In 1973 a newspaper reported an unusual disturbance at a Pakistani wedding. The bride turned on the guests in the wedding party and felled her father-in-law with a bottle of whisky, fracturing his skull. She then set about her father and locked her mother in the toilet before running into the street, stealing the bridegroom's car and crashing it. All he could say, as she disappeared into the crowd, was, "This is the first time she has expressed any emotion towards me."

from *Comic Speeches for Social Occasions*

*

"When Menachem Teitelbaum married Brucha Meisels in December 1984, 150 buses transported more than twenty thousand guests to the pre-wedding reception at Nassau Coliseum, home of the New York Islanders ice hockey team, but only eight thousand went to the sit-down dinner afterwards."

from *The Guinness Book of Marriage*

*

One of the longest engagements lasted 44 years, and is noted by Martin Lewis in ". . . And finally" "She was 68 and he a sprightly 72 when they finally made it to the altar." By which time they were on their fourth engagement ring - the others having worn through!

. . . I'D ALSO LIKE TO SAY HOW DELIRIOUSLY AND EMOTIONALLY OVERWHELMED KIM AND I WERE WITH THE EIGHTY-SIX EMBROIDERED MONOGRAMMED NAPKINS FROM AUNT EDNA . . .

"If it were not for the presents, an elopement would be preferable."

GEORGE ADE

I'M JUST TOSSING UP TO SEE WHICH SEVEN TOASTERS
WE TAKE BACK...

*YOU CANNOT PUT A SEASON TICKET FOR YOUR TEAM
ON OUR WEDDING LIST!*

The happy Chicago couple had arranged a display of their wedding presents at the reception for their guests to admire. In central position grandly displayed was an envelope containing a "million dollar check" which was the present from the bride's father. Standing in front of it was a man doubled up with laughter.

"Who on earth is that?" asked the groom.

"Oh, just Daddy's bank manager," explained the bride.

WIFE IN TRAINING

The young bride was overcome with embarrassment as she and her groom approached the hotel on their wedding night.

"I don't want all the other guests to know that we're on our honeymoon - how can we make everyone think that we've been married for years?"

"That's simple, darling," replied her husband, "but do you think you can manage both suitcases?"

*

Abdul Hamassa, seventy-eight, of Alexandria, Eygpt, asked for a divorce from his latest wife on the grounds that the bride behaved too childishly. The court threw the case out. Said the judge: "Abdul must have known what to expect when he married the 'woman' who had just turned eleven."

*

The new bride was taking a course in home economics.

"What have you learned to cook?" asked her husband.

"Oh, we haven't got as far as cooking," she replied. "We're only up to thawing."

ROY BOLITHO

*

I KNOW WE PROMISED FATHER WE'D CUT DOWN ON EXPENSES MALCOLM, BUT...

"Marriage is like panty-hose. It depends on what you put into it."

PHYLLIS SCHLAFLY

*

"Never go to bed mad. Stay up and fight."

PHYLLIS DILLER

*

In a marital dispute the partner who apologizes always has the last word.

*

"Keep thy eyes wide open before marriage and half shut afterward."

THOMAS FULLER

DON'T PANIC, BUT I THINK I SPOTTED YOUR MOTHER

IN THE NON-SMOKERS...

THE BIRDS AND THE BEES

The bride had got a little drunk and was having some difficulty in making her speech of thanks for all the wonderful wedding gifts.

At the end of her speech she pointed rather unsteadily to an electric coffee percolator, and said: "And finally I'd like to thank my husband's parents for giving me such a lovely perky copulator."

KEVIN GOLDSTEIN-JACKSON, from *Joke after Joke after Joke*

*

A mother and daughter are talking on the eve of the daughter's wedding. The daughter asks, "But will he still respect me after we are married?" The mother answers, "Well dear, that's up to you. But take my advice and never let him see you totally naked. I've never let your father see me without something on, and he has respected me for over thirty years of marriage."

About six months after the wedding, the son-in-law speaks to the mother. "Is there something

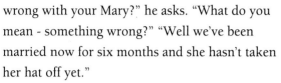

wrong with your Mary?" he asks. "What do you mean - something wrong?" "Well we've been married now for six months and she hasn't taken her hat off yet."

BARRY WOGAN, from *Wedding Speeches and Jokes*

MOTHER TOLD ME WHAT TO EXPECT TONIGHT BUT, QUITE FRANKLY, I DIDN'T BELIEVE HER...

I KNOW YOU ENJOYED THE CEREMONY, BUT YOU CAN

TAKE IT OFF NOW...

Groom: "Would you be very annoyed with me if I confess that all my upper teeth are false?"

Bride: "Not at all, darling. At least I can now relax and take off my wig, inflatable bra, glass eye and artificial leg."

KEVIN GOLDSTEIN-JACKSON, from *Joke after Joke after Joke*

*

"Why does a woman work ten years to change a man's habits and then complain that he's not the man she married?"

BARBRA STREISAND

*

"Did you hear the one about the woman who married her electrician and complained that on her wedding night three of them turned up - one to estimate the job, one to do it and one to pick up the bits in the morning."

from *The 2 Ronnies - The Best of the Ronnies' Dialogue*

*

"You know when the honeymoon is over - it's when the dog brings your slippers and your wife barks at you."

ROY BOLITHO

*

"When a girl marries, she exchanges the attentions of many men for the inattention of one."

HELEN ROWLAND

*

"Before marriage a man will lie awake all night thinking about something you said; after marriage he will fall asleep before you have finished saying it!"

HELEN ROWLAND

*

It begins with a prince kissing an angel.
It ends with a baldheaded man looking across the table at a fat woman.

*

It begins when you sink into his arms; and ends with your arms in his sink.

GOSH! WHAT A DAY - I'M TIRED OUT. SEE YOU IN

THE MORNING, LOVE...